Albert Einstein

Libby Romero

NATIONAL
GEOGRAPHIC

Washington, D.C.

For Seth and Ryan. Love you! —L.R.

Trade paperback ISBN:
978-1-4263-2536-6
Reinforced library binding ISBN:
978-1-4263-2537-3

The author and publisher gratefully acknowledge the expert content review of this book by Dr. Dennis Lehmkuhl, scientific editor of the Einstein Papers Project, California Institute of Technology, and the literacy review of this book by Mariam Jean Dreher, professor of reading education, University of Maryland, College Park.

Author's Note

Albert Einstein made many notable contributions to the scientific community. In an effort to help young readers understand Einstein and his work, the author has focused on major events in his life and simplified the science as much as possible. To learn more about this amazing man, read *Genius: A Photobiography of Albert Einstein,* by Marfé Ferguson Delano (National Geographic Society, 2005).

Photo Credits

GI = Getty Images; SS = Shutterstock; TGC: The Granger Collection, New York
Cover, Library of Congress Prints and Photographs Division; (CTR), Heritage Image Partnership/Alamy; Vocabulary box (throughout), XyJluraH/SS; Top border (throughout), watchara/SS; 1 (CTR), Corbis; 3 (LO RT), ullstein bild/GI; 5 (LE), Ralph Morse/The LIFE Picture Collection/GI; 5 (UP), Arguelles/Transcendental Graphics/GI; 6 (LE), TGC; 6 (RT), TGC; 7 (UP), World History Archive/Alamy; 8 (CTR), World History Archive/Alamy; 8 (LO), UIG/GI; 9 (RT), UIG/GI; 10 (UP), ullstein bild/GI; 10 (LO), De Agostini/GI; 11 (UP RT), Fanfo/SS; 11 (CTR), Hulton Archive/GI; 11 (LO), Alinari/GI; 12 (UP), TGC; 13 (LO), ullstein bild/GI; 14, NG Maps; 15 (LO RT), Alamy; 16 (UP), World History Archive/Alamy; 17 (LO RT), Press Select/Alamy; 18 (LO), Everett Collection/Alamy; 19 (UP), ullstein bild/TGC; 20 (LO RT), Sueddeutsche Zeitung Photo/Alamy; 21 (CTR), TGC; 21 (LO LE), Photodisc; 22 (UP), ullstein bild/Granger Collection, New York; 22 (LO), Yay! Design; 23 (LO), Ros Drinkwater/Alamy; 24 (UP), Willyam Bradberry/SS; 24 (CTR), Deco/Alamy; 25 (LO RT), INTERFOTO/Alamy; 27 (CTR), Lachina; 28 (LO), Everett Historical/SS; 29 (UP LE), Georgios Kollidas/SS; 29 (LO RT), Chronicle/Alamy; 29 (LO), TGC; 29 (LO LE), Nicku/SS; 29 (UP RT), Georgios Kollidas/SS; 30 (UP LE), David Silverman/GI; 30 (CTR RT), UIG/GI; 30 (LO LE), AFP/GI; 31 (UP LE), Photographer's Choice/GI; 31 (CTR RT), Ernst Haas/GI; 31 (CTR LE), New York Times Co./GI; 31 (LO), TGC; 32 (CTR), ullstein bild/Granger Collection, New York; 33 (UP), Peter van Evert/Alamy; 34 (CTR), Bettmann/GI; 35 (UP), Yay! Design; 36-37 (UP), Yay! Design; 37 (CTR), AAR Studio/SS; 38 (UP), UIG/GI; 39 (UP RT), Akademie/Alamy; 39 (LO), Pictorial Press Ltd/Alamy; 40 (CTR LE), World History Archive/Alamy; 41 (CTR), Oliver Morris/GI; 42 (UP), Saul Loeb/AFP/GI; 42-43 (CTR), EtiAmmos/SS; 43 (CTR), Bettmann/GI; 44 (UP), ilolab/SS; 44 (CTR), ullstein bild/GI; 44 (LO), TGC; 45 (UP LE), TGC; 45 (UP RT), SPL/Science Source; 45 (CTR LE), Akademie/Alamy; 45 (LO RT), Agsandrew/Dreamstime; 46 (UP), Brand X/GI; 46 (CTR LE), Willyam Bradberry/SS; 46 (CTR RT), Deco/Alamy; 46 (LO LE), Science Photo Library/GI; 46 (LO RT), AAR Studio/SS; 47 (UP LE), David Silverman/GI; 47 (UP RT), Yay! Design; 47 (CTR LE), Yay! Design; 47 (CTR RT), SPL/Science Source; 47 (LO LE), Lachina; 47 (LO RT), TGC

National Geographic supports K–12 educators with ELA Common Core Resources.
Visit natgeoed.org/commoncore for more information.

Printed in the United States of America
16/WOR/1

Table of Contents

Who Was Albert Einstein?   4

Growing Up in Germany   6

In His Time   10

Educating Einstein   12

Miracle Year   20

6 Cool Facts About Einstein   30

Research and Reward   32

A Final Quest   40

Quiz Whiz   44

Glossary   46

Index   48

Who Was Albert Einstein?

Albert Einstein was a scientist. He came up with new ideas about time and space. He formed new theories about how the universe works.

Einstein's ideas made him famous and changed what people thought about the universe.

His ideas also led to new types of science. Because of this, people called Einstein a genius (JEAN-yus). His ideas are still important today.

Word to Know

THEORY: An idea that is used to predict or explain something

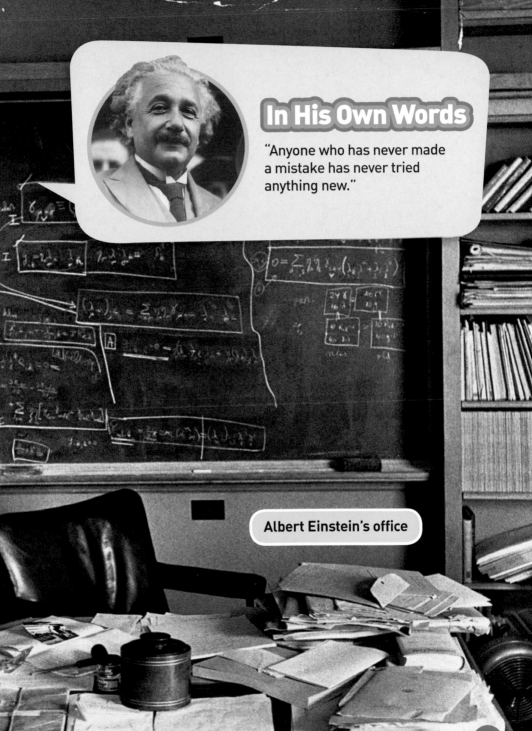

In His Own Words

"Anyone who has never made a mistake has never tried anything new."

Albert Einstein's office

Growing Up in Germany

Albert Einstein was born in Ulm, Germany, on March 14, 1879. His father, Hermann, was a businessman. His mother, Pauline, loved music. She passed this love on to Einstein and his younger sister, Maja (MY-yah).

Einstein's parents

This photo shows Einstein at four years old.

When Einstein was born, his mother worried because his head was large. He looked different from other babies. And then, he didn't start to speak when he should have. A child usually says a few simple words by his or her first birthday. Einstein did not speak until he was between two and three years old.

Einstein's sister, Maja, was two years younger than him.

In His Own Words

"I have no special talents. I am only passionately curious."

But Einstein's parents had no reason to worry. He was smart. He was also very curious.

Einstein's lifelong curiosity about science started when he was five. His father gave him a magnetic compass. Einstein played with the compass. When he turned it in different directions, he noticed that the needle always pointed north.

Young Einstein did not understand why this happened. He imagined that an invisible force was controlling the needle. For the rest of his life, he remembered that compass and the invisible force.

a compass

In His Time

Einstein grew up in Germany during the 1880s. Back then, many things were different from how they are today.

NEWS: People didn't have radios or TVs during the 1880s. Instead, they read newspapers and magazines to get their news.

TOYS: German craftsmen carved and painted wooden toys. Factories made dolls, mechanical toys, and construction sets.

FOOD: There were no refrigerators. People smoked, cured, and pickled foods that they stored and ate during the winter.

CLOTHING: The sailor suit was one of the most popular styles of clothing for both boys and girls.

TRANSPORTATION: There were railroads, but no cars or planes. Most people walked or used horses to get around. In some cities, there were streetcar systems.

Ernst Drucker-Theater

Educating Einstein

In 1889, Einstein attended school in Munich, Germany. This photo shows him (circled) with his classmates.

Einstein started school when he was six. As a boy, he loved to explore. He also liked to think for himself. His family had moved to Munich, Germany. Schools there were strict. Teachers told students what and how to think. Because of this, Einstein didn't like school.

But he did love to learn. Einstein borrowed books and taught himself math and science at home. He fell in love with physics. That's the science of energy, matter, and movement.

Word to Know

MATTER: Anything that has mass and takes up space

Understanding Mass

Mass is the amount of matter in an object. Larger objects tend to have more mass than smaller objects. But smaller objects can have more mass if the particles of matter in them are packed more closely together.

a portrait of Einstein at 14 years old

A Global Citizen

Einstein spent most of his life in central Europe. After he was born, his family moved to Munich, Germany. Then they moved to Milan, Italy. He finished high school in Aarau, Switzerland, and attended university in Zurich, Switzerland. He also lived in Bern, Switzerland; Prague, Czech Republic (which was then part of the Austro-Hungarian Empire); and Berlin, Germany, before moving to the United States in 1933.

When Einstein was 15, his family moved to Milan, Italy. Einstein stayed in Munich to finish school. But soon he left to join his family.

Einstein's parents were worried because he had left school. He promised to teach himself at home and go to a university in the fall. Unfortunately, Einstein studied only subjects he liked and ignored everything else.

Einstein went to Zurich, Switzerland. He took and failed the university's entrance exam. But the university director was impressed. He told Einstein to attend a nearby high school for a year and reapply.

an illustration of a street in Milan, Italy, painted during 1890–1900

Einstein (circled) with his graduation class in Aarau, Switzerland

The new school was the perfect place for a budding scientist. Teachers wanted students to think about things in new ways. Also, the school had a great physics laboratory for students to use.

At this time, Einstein started to think about problems. He tried to picture the solution in his head. He called these experiences "thought experiments." His first thought experiment was about light. He asked himself: *What would it be like if you could ride on a beam of light?*

That's a FACT! Einstein's best theories didn't come from working in a laboratory. They were ideas he imagined.

In His Own Words

"Imagination is more important than knowledge."

Einstein finished high school one year later. Then he was accepted into the university. Einstein wanted to learn the latest scientific theories. But the university mostly taught ideas that people had accepted for a long time.

Einstein attended the Swiss Federal Institute of Technology in Zurich, also called Zurich Polytechnic. It is the large building on the hill.

a photo of Albert Einstein working in the patent office in 1905, at age 26

Einstein struggled to graduate from the university. After he did, it took two years for him to get a steady job. The job was in a patent office. He thought his new job was interesting. It also gave him lots of time to think about science.

Word to Know

PATENT: An official paper that gives people rights to new inventions for a period of time

Miracle Year

Three years later, in 1905, Einstein was still working in the patent office. He did thought experiments in his free time. He wrote about his ideas in four papers. He published them in an important German scientific journal called *Annalen der Physik* (Annals of Physics). These ideas would change science forever.

That same year, Einstein earned his doctoral degree from the University of Zurich. People were amazed by what Einstein had done in such a short period of time. They called 1905 his "miracle year." He was only 26 years old.

During his "miracle year," Einstein lived with his first wife, Mileva.

3. Zur Elektrodynamik bewegter Körper; von A. Einstein.

Daß die Elektrodynamik Maxwells — wie dieselbe gegenwärtig aufgefaßt zu werden pflegt — in ihrer Anwendung auf bewegte Körper zu Asymmetrien führt, welche den Phänomenen nicht anzuhaften scheinen, ist bekannt. Man denke z. B. an die elektrodynamische Wechselwirkung zwischen einem Magneten und einem Leiter. Das beobachtbare Phänomen hängt hier nur ab von der Relativbewegung von Leiter und Magnet, ... ichen Auffassung die beiden Fälle, daß ... re dieser Körper der bewegte sei, streng ... sind. Bewegt sich nämlich der Magnet ... entsteht in der Umgebung des Magneten ... von gewissem Energiewerte, welches an den Orten, wo sich Teile des Leiters befinden, einen Strom erzeugt. Ruht aber der Magnet und bewegt sich der Leiter, so entsteht in der Umgebung des Magneten kein elektrisches Feld, dagegen im Leiter eine elektromotorische Kraft, welcher an sich keine Energie entspricht, die aber — Gleichheit der Relativbewegung bei den beiden ins Auge gefaßten Fällen vorausgesetzt — zu elektrischen Strömen von derselben Größe und demselben Verlaufe Veranlassung gibt, wie im ersten Falle die elektrischen Kräfte.

Beispiele ähnlicher Art, sowie die mißlungenen Versuche, eine Bewegung der Erde relativ zum „Lichtmedium" zu konstatieren, führen zu der Vermutung, daß dem Begriffe der ... der Mechanik, sondern auch in ... en ent- ... steme, ... h die ... n, wie ... Wir ... Prinzip ... ng er- ... ägliche

This is the beginning of one of Einstein's papers, published in his "miracle year."

Academic Publishing

Scientists, researchers, and scholars often publish detailed papers about their work. Other people working in their fields read the papers. People can comment on the ideas. Some may even find a way to use the new ideas in their own work.

First Paper: Light

In his first paper of 1905, Einstein wrote about light. Most people at the time believed that light was a wave of energy. Einstein argued that light was actually a stream of tiny particles.

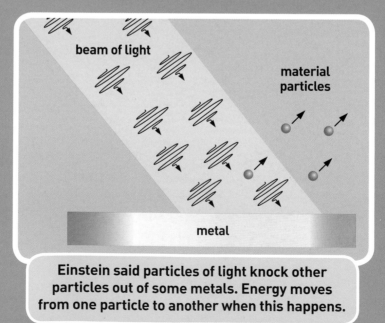

beam of light

material particles

metal

Einstein said particles of light knock other particles out of some metals. Energy moves from one particle to another when this happens.

Einstein's idea led to a new type of science called "quantum physics." People now use the ideas from quantum physics to make things like televisions and computer chips.

the home in Bern, Switzerland, where Einstein and Mileva lived during his "miracle year"

an illustration of atoms and molecules in water

Second Paper: Atoms

In his second paper of 1905, Einstein made a case for what other scientists had long suspected: Atoms and molecules are real.

Einstein found new evidence for this idea after thinking about how tiny particles move in water. Other scientists had seen this movement through microscopes. However, they could not explain how the particles moved.

Einstein imagined that the objects in water were banging against atoms and molecules. He used math to figure out *how* the objects would move. People tested his idea. The objects moved exactly as he had predicted.

Words to Know

ATOM: A tiny part of a whole piece of matter

MOLECULE: Two or more atoms joined together

PREDICT: To tell something that will happen in the future

a microscope from the 1920s

Third Paper: Time and Space

With his third paper of 1905, Einstein changed how people thought about time and space. People had thought that time always moved at the same speed for everyone. They thought that distances people experience must also be the same.

Einstein said that was not true. He assumed that no matter how fast someone is moving, the speed of light stays the same. But for everything else, speed changes based on how fast the person watching is moving.

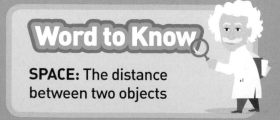

Word to Know

SPACE: The distance between two objects

A girl is on a moving train. She throws a ball. To her, the ball looks like it's moving slower than it looks to the boy on the ground. She shines a light. The beam of light looks like it is traveling at the same speed to both the boy and the girl.

Einstein did a thought experiment. He imagined he was riding on a beam of light. He realized that time would seem one way to him and another way to someone moving at a different speed. So would distance. Other scientists tested his idea. They said Einstein was right.

Fourth Paper: Matter and Energy

In his fourth paper of 1905, Einstein wrote about the relationship between energy and matter. He said that energy and matter are two forms of the same thing. And once again, he used math to show how his idea worked.

Einstein created an equation. It said that energy (E) is equal to the mass (m) of an object multiplied by the speed of light squared (c^2). Using Einstein's idea, other scientists found a way to release the energy in matter. They built reactors that supplied energy. They also built powerful bombs.

Word to Know

EQUATION: A mathematical statement that says two amounts are equal, such as $1 + 2 = 3$

the first atomic bomb explosion

Einstein's Ideas

Einstein admired the ideas of earlier scientists. He used ideas from four scientists to create new ideas about time and space. He always gave credit to Galileo Galilei (1564–1642); Isaac Newton (1642–1727); James Clerk Maxwell (1831–1879); and Hendrik Antoon Lorentz (1835–1928).

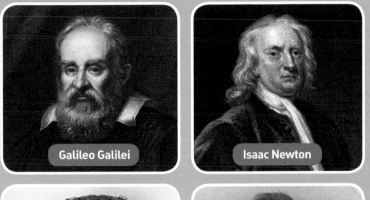

Galileo Galilei

Isaac Newton

James Clerk Maxwell

Hendrik Antoon Lorentz

That's a FACT!

$$\left(E = mc^2\right)$$

Einstein's formula $E = mc^2$ was simple. But it has become one of the most famous mathematical statements ever written. This is the equation in Einstein's handwriting.

6 COOL FACTS
About Einstein

1 Einstein helped raise money to support the United States in World War II. He auctioned a handwritten copy of one of his 1905 papers. It sold for $6.5 million.

2 People consider Albert Einstein to be the most important scientist of the 20th century.

3 Einstein was a talented violin player. Once, he said he would have become a musician if he had not been a scientist.

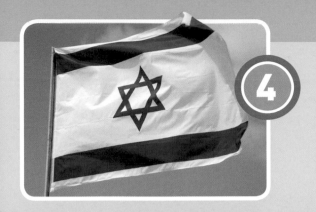

4

In 1952, the nation of Israel asked Einstein to become its second president. He turned down the offer.

Albert Einstein refused to wear socks because they got holes in them.

5

Elnstein was married twice. He had one daughter, whom he never met. He had two sons and two stepdaughters.

Einstein and his second wife, Elsa, with his stepdaughter Margot

6

Einstein's first wife, Mileva, with their sons Eduard (left) and Hans Albert (right)

Research and Reward

Einstein's ideas stirred up discussions among scientists. Some didn't think he was right. But others praised him. Einstein had found answers to problems they had not been able to solve.

His ideas also made him famous. In 1909, he started teaching at a university. Soon, other universities wanted the brilliant scientist to teach at and bring fame to their schools.

That's a FACT! In 1912, Einstein became a professor at Zurich Polytechnic, where he had failed the entrance exam years earlier.

One of the universities where Einstein taught was Leiden University in the Netherlands.

But teaching left Einstein with little time to think about new ideas. So in 1914, he became the director of a research institute in Berlin, Germany. He was still a professor, but he didn't have to teach. He had time to focus on ideas and talk to other scientists.

In 1915, Einstein wrote his masterpiece. He called it the "general theory of relativity." People always thought of gravity as a force that pulls two things together. In his theory, Einstein linked that idea of gravity with his new ideas about space and time.

His former teacher Hermann Minkowski had studied one of Einstein's 1905 papers. He said Einstein's ideas suggested that space and time are joined together to create something called "spacetime."

Hermann Minkowski

Word to Know

GRAVITY: The force of attraction between all objects with mass in the universe. It's what causes objects with less mass to move toward or around objects with more mass.

Understanding General Relativity

Imagine spacetime as a grid. According to Einstein, without matter, that grid is flat. But when matter is present, the spacetime grid bends. This curve makes objects move toward each other. And that is what we see as gravity.

Einstein used spacetime to form the general theory of relativity. It says that even when pulled by gravity, objects move on the straightest possible paths through spacetime. The more matter that is present, the more spacetime is bent. It's like when a ball is dropped into a bedsheet, and it bends the sheet.

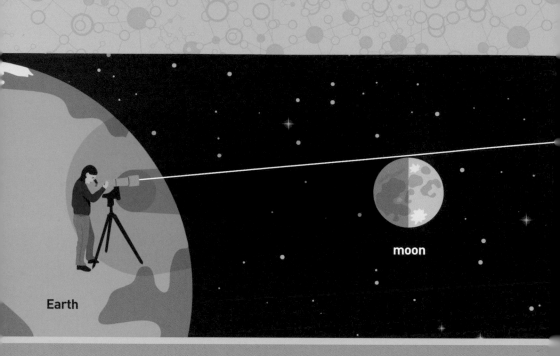

moon

Earth

Based on his new theory, Einstein predicted that starlight would bend as it passed the sun. He said people could confirm his idea during a solar eclipse. Then, the moon's shadow would fall on Earth and the sun's glare would be out of the way. People could see and measure light from stars located out beyond the sun.

That's a FACT! Other scientists studied Einstein's theory. It helped them figure out how the universe formed. Their idea is called the big bang theory.

apparent position

true position

sun

Einstein's Prediction About Starlight

Einstein said the sun changes spacetime around it. He predicted this would make stars look like they were in one place. In reality, they are located in a different part of the sky. In May 1919, British astronomers tested Einstein's idea during a total eclipse of the sun. He was right. Starlight bent as it passed by the sun.

Word to Know

SOLAR ECLIPSE: A time when the moon moves between Earth and the sun, blocking sunlight from reaching Earth

Einstein went to the White House and met with U.S. president Warren Harding in 1921.

Newspapers around the world wrote about Einstein and his ideas. Now, scientists weren't the only ones who knew who he was. Movie stars wanted to meet him. Many people recognized him and talked about his ideas.

Then, in 1922, Einstein
was awarded the 1921
Nobel Prize in Physics.
This award honors the best
new ideas in science. Einstein
did not get the award for his ideas about time
and space. The award committee thought
that people disagreed too much about those
ideas. Instead, they honored his overall work
in physics. They noted his discoveries about
particles of light.

Thousands of people lined the streets
of New York City when Einstein first
visited the United States in 1921.

A Final Quest

Beginning in 1922, Einstein started to focus on a new idea. He thought that a single theory could explain how everything in the universe works together. If he found the right theory, he thought, it might also explain the structure of matter. He spent the rest of his life working on this problem.

That's a FACT! Einstein loved to sail. Being on the water gave him time to think.

1879
born in Ulm, Germany, on March 14

1880
family moves to Munich

1895
joins family in Milan

1900
graduates from university

Many scientists thought Einstein was wasting his time. But Einstein thought he could find the answer. If not, he believed that someone else would.

A Safe Place

In 1932, Einstein accepted a position at Princeton University in Princeton, New Jersey, U.S.A. In 1933, he made the United States his new home. At that time, Germany was not a safe place for him to live. Einstein was Jewish, and many Germans did not trust Jewish people. Einstein thought the United States would be a safer place to live, work, and think. He was right. World War II started in 1939. Jewish people in Germany were no longer safe.

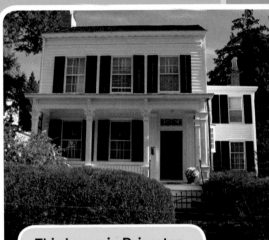

This house in Princeton, New Jersey, was Einstein's home from 1936 until he died in 1955.

1902
begins working in patent office

1905
has "miracle year"

1909
becomes university professor

1914
becomes director of research institute in Berlin

In 1916, Einstein predicted that gravity waves exist. In 2016, scientists announced that they had confirmed Einstein's prediction. They detected ripples in spacetime caused by the collision of two black holes. This discovery opened a new way to study the universe.

Einstein died in Princeton, New Jersey, on April 18, 1955. Even in his last days, he worked on his dream of a "theory of everything." He never found the answer.

Scientists have continued to try to solve Einstein's puzzle. They have made progress. But for now, his final theory still hasn't been confirmed.

1915
publishes general theory of relativity

1919
receives confirmation from scientists that his ideas about starlight bending are right

1922
awarded 1921 Nobel Prize

In His Own Words

"I never think of the future. It comes soon enough."

1932

accepts position at Princeton University

1933

moves to U.S.

1940

becomes a U.S. citizen

1955

dies in Princeton, New Jersey, on April 18

QUIZ WHIZ

How much do you know about Albert Einstein? After reading this book, probably a lot! Take this quiz and find out.

Answers are at the bottom of page 45.

1

Where was Albert Einstein born?

A. United States
B. Germany
C. Switzerland
D. England

2

When Einstein was a boy, he fell in love with this subject:

A. biology
B. chemistry
C. physics
D. geology

What is a theory?

A. an idea that is used to predict or explain something
B. a very small piece of matter
C. a force that pulls things together
D. anything that has mass and takes up space

3

4

Albert Einstein became interested in science after his father _____.

A. read him a book
B. took him to school
C. gave him a compass
D. showed him the stars

5

Which year is called Einstein's "miracle year"?

A. 1879
B. 1905
C. 1922
D. 1955

6

Albert Einstein received the Nobel Prize mostly for his ideas about _____.

A. space and time
B. gravity
C. particles of light
D. solar eclipses

7

Which of Einstein's ideas are scientists still trying to develop?

A. the theory of light particles
B. the theory of spacetime
C. the theory of gravity
D. the theory of everything

Glossary

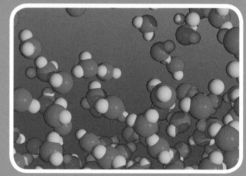

ATOM: A tiny part of a whole piece of matter

MATTER: Anything that has mass and takes up space

MOLECULE: Two or more atoms joined together

PREDICT: To tell something that will happen in the future

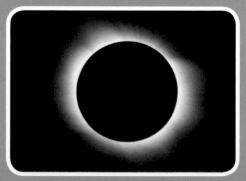

SOLAR ECLIPSE: A time when the moon moves between Earth and the sun, blocking sunlight from reaching Earth

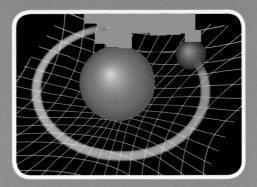

EQUATION: A mathematical statement that says two amounts are equal, such as 1 + 2 = 3

GRAVITY: The force of attraction between all objects with mass in the universe. It's what causes objects with less mass to move toward or around objects with more mass.

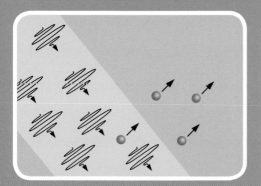

PARTICLE: A very small piece of matter

PATENT: An official paper that gives people rights to new inventions for a period of time

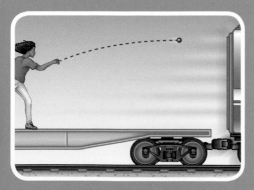

SPACE: The distance between two objects

THEORY: An idea that is used to predict or explain something

Index

Boldface indicates illustrations.

A

Atomic bombs 28, **28–29**
Atoms **24**, 24–25, 46, **46**

C

Compass 9, **9**

E

E = mc² 28–29, **29**
Eclipses, solar 36, **36–37**, 46, **46**
Einstein, Albert
    childhood 6–15, **7, 8, 13**
    cool facts 30–31, **30–31**
    curiosity 8, 9, 22
    education **12**, 12–20, **16**
    fame 32, 38, **38**, **39**
    family **6**, 6–7, **8**, **20**, 31, **31**
    final quest 40–43
    imagination 9, 17, 25, 27
    love of music 6, 30, **30**
    miracle year 20–29
    Nobel Prize 39, **39**
    patent office job **19**, 19–20
    research **4–5, 32**, 32–39
    sailing 40, **40**
Einstein, Eduard (son) 31, **31**
Einstein, Elsa (wife) 31, **31**
Einstein, Hans Albert (son) 31, **31**
Einstein, Hermann (father) 6, **6**
Einstein, Maja (sister) 6, **8**
Einstein, Mileva (wife) **20, 23**, 31, **31**
Einstein, Pauline (mother) **6**, 6–7
Energy and matter 28–29
Equations 28, 47, **47**

G

Galilei, Galileo 29, **29**
General theory of relativity 34–37, **35**
Glossary 46–47, **46–47**
Gravity 34–35, 42, 47, **47**

H

Harding, Warren 38, **38**

I

Israel 31, **31**

L

Light 22, **22**, 26–27, 39
Lorentz, Hendrik Antoon 29, **29**

M

Magnetism 9, **9**
Map 14
Mass 13, 28, 34, 46, 47
Matter 13, 28–29, 46, **46**
Maxwell, James Clerk 29, **29**
Microscopes 25, **25**
Minkowski, Hermann 34, **34**
Molecules **24**, 24–25, 46, **46**

N

Newton, Isaac 29, **29**
Nobel Prize in Physics 39, **39**

P

Particles 22, **22**, 23, **24**, 25, 47, **47**
Patent office **19**, 19–20, 47, **47**
Physics 13, 20–29
Prediction 25, 46, **46**

Q

Quantum physics 23
Quiz 44–45, **44–45**

R

Relativity 34–37, **35**

S

Solar eclipses 36, **36–37**, 46, **46**
Space 26–27, 34, 47, **47**
Spacetime 34–37
Speed of light 26–27
Starlight 36–37, **37**

T

Theory, definition of 4, 17, 47, **47**
Theory of everything 40–42
Theory of relativity 34–37, **35**
Thought experiments 17, 27
Time and space 26–27, 34

W

Water, particles in **24**, 25
World War II 30, 41

3